USING NAVY RECORDS

Public Record Office
Pocket Guides to Family History

Getting Started in Family History

Using Birth, Marriage and Death Records

Using Census Returns

Using Wills

Using Army Records

Using Navy Records

USING NAVY RECORDS

PUBLIC RECORD OFFICE

Public Record Office
Richmond
Surrey
TW9 4DU

ISBN 1 873162 92 8

A catalogue card for this book
is available from the British Library

Front cover: an officer of HMS *Calliope*, 1890
(PRO COPY 1/400)

Printed by Cromwell Press Ltd, Trowbridge, Wilts.

CONTENTS

INTRODUCTION

There is a huge body of records available mainly at the Public Record Office (PRO) for searching to find an ancestor who was in the Navy. Records exist by rank and by ship, but there is no single index by name to help you locate your ancestor easily. Unless you already know the ship on which your ancestor served at a specific time you must be prepared to be tenacious in your searching. It is the large number of fragmentary records that makes searching so difficult.

When you do find an ancestor, you will discover a wealth of detail evocative of an adventurous life. You can find a record of what your ancestor looked like, kept to identify him in case of death or desertion. You can also find which ships he served on, where he went, and details of his career including punishments and promotions.

ORIGINS OF THE NAVY

The origins of the Navy lie in the merchant shipping of medieval England. The king owned his own ships but could also call upon the merchant fleet as the need arose. Successive kings granted trading privileges to a group of five ports on the south coast, known as the Cinque Ports. Part of the return on the privileges was the ability to call upon them for help in defence of English maritime interests. At this time, and for many years afterwards, it was possible to convert a ship easily between trading and defensive use. This was done as the need arose, more or less on the personal authority of the king, so there is a lack of structure to the records, which makes searching them more difficult.

The beginnings of a structured navy can be traced from the time of the Tudors. Henry VII owned personally a fleet of seven ships, which were used for trading as well as defence, and this fleet was greatly expanded by Henry VIII. The Tudors were quick to grasp the implications of the discoveries of the New World and the importance for the British Isles of having a strong navy to defend their interests and protect them from attack by rival European countries. Henry VIII set up an organisation known as the Navy Board to oversee the royal fleet, and also appointed a small number of officers to take charge of the ships. Advances were made in the design of the ships and their armaments were built up, so that by the time the Spanish Armada set sail in 1588 the Royal Navy was strong enough to meet it.

RECRUITMENT

The cost of manning a sailing ship was high. The work of managing the sails was labour-intensive and by 1816 the largest ships in the Royal Navy needed nearly a thousand men. In times of war huge numbers of men were needed, up to 20,000. In peacetime the practice continued right up to the mid-19th century of decommissioning the majority of ships so that only a skeleton staff remained. Sailors were paid only for the periods they spent working and the length of each period depended on the nature of the service being undertaken. The career of a typical ordinary seaman was episodic, with service in the Navy being interspersed with unemployment or service on merchant ships. The episodic nature of navy service is reflected in the records. There was no centralised monitoring of the progress of a sailor's career. Individual captains with their own objectives carried out recruitment. They organised their men in their own way, using their own preferences (known as ratings) for naming and structuring the ranks, and kept their own records for the ships under their command.

Life on board ship for ordinary seamen was harsh and dangerous. The cramped and ill-ventilated accommodation was a breeding ground for illness. Food and water were spoiled within a few days of leaving shore, and even after the cause of scurvy had been discovered to be lack of anti-scorbutic acid, the availability of the fresh produce that contained it depended on great ingenuity on the part of the captain and the purser of each ship. Apart from the dangers of war and sickness, there was a constant wastage of men lost overboard or killed or maimed by falling from the rigging. In addition punishments were numerous and particularly cruel even for the time. The

I hereby certify that my son, *John James Noblett*, has my full consent (being himself willing) to enter Her Majesty's Navy for a period of Ten Years' Continuous and General Service, from the age of 18, in addition to whatever period may be necessary until he attain that age, agreeably to Her Majesty's Order in Council, dated 1st April, '53, and the Admiralty Regulations of the 14th June, '53, relating thereto. And I also declare that he has never had fits. *nor been an inmate of a reformatory*

Witness our hands at *Brockhurst*

26th day of *September* 18*71*

Date of Boy's Birth, *13th September 1856*

Parent's Signature, { or, if dead, nearest relative } *Amelia Noblett*

Boy's Signature of consent, and who further declares that he is not Indentured as an apprentice. *John Noblett James*

Witness, *H J Martin*

G [1789] 8000 5/66

Parental consent form for John Noblett to enter
a continuous service engagement with the Navy
at the age of 18, 1871 (PRO ADM 139/975)

practice of flogging was not suspended in the Navy until 1871, and that suspension was only during peacetime. On top of all this the men had to endure rates of pay that were generally low throughout the period and delays in payment, often for months and sometimes years.

All in all there was little incentive for ordinary men to join the Navy, apart from a small core of a few thousand men who chose it for a career and often sought advancement through it. In times of war when the need for men rose rapidly there were great shortages. The use of press gangs to force men into service did not die out until the early 19th century. If men saw an opportunity they would often desert (though this was punishable by death). Desertion was so common that you will find a separate column for it in many muster books and pay rolls.

A regular scheme of entrance into the Navy was not instituted until the Continuous Service Act was passed in 1853. This introduced a ten year period of continuous service starting at 18 years of age, with an increase in pay and prospects and a right to a pension after 20 years' service. Many seamen already in service were offered the same terms of employment so that after this point it becomes much easier to trace them through the Continuous Service Engagement Books described on pp. 31–5.

In 1903 an alternative short term of service was introduced. This system required service of only five or seven years, with a commitment to the Royal Fleet Reserve for a further seven or five years respectively to make the complete service up to twelve years.

OFFICERS

Appointment to the higher ranks of officers in the Royal Navy was only by commission until 1860. This was a system that originated with the crown and remained closely connected with the monarchs of the day until the time of Queen Victoria. For example, the future William IV was sent to join the Navy at 14 years old. Commissions were purchased by the wealthy under the patronage of a small circle of influential people. In addition, minimum requirements for a lieutenant's commission were established in the late 18th century, including a minimum age and length of time spent at sea. Nearly all admirals, captains, commanders and lieutenants were appointed through the influence of their connections, though it was possible for men of outstanding ability to rise through the ranks, especially in wartime.

There were also some officers aboard ship who were appointed by warrant by the captain to provide specialist skills. These included, for instance, surgeons, engineers and gunners. They were likely either to hold a professional qualification or to have served an apprenticeship. Some training records of these officers survive. Other officers appointed by warrant had skills required for the running and maintenance of the ship, such as masters, boatswains and midshipmen. These were known as 'standing officers' because they remained with the ship to maintain it even while it was out of commission. In the reorganisations of the 19th century most of these officers were given commissions, leaving only three warrant ranks by 1847. Since the manning of his ship was the responsibility of the captain, the scope of his patronage was wide. A popular captain was able to maintain a relatively stable core crew from voyage to voyage.

Although buying a commission was expensive and officers' pay was not high, the Navy was a popular profession amongst the wealthy. It was noble and adventurous, and could be lucrative on assignments where enemy cargo was seized and divided among the crew as prize money. There were often more commissioned officers than posts available during peacetime so a system of half pay was introduced to retain officers between engagements.

WHERE TO GO TO SEARCH

There are numerous different types of record surviving that may mention individuals in the Royal Navy. The largest collection of interest to family historians is held at the Public Record Office, Kew. This Pocket Guide describes their main characteristics, but does not have space to list them all by name, although the table on pp. 20–23 provides a summary. You can find a more detailed description in Roger, *Naval Records for Genealogists*. The Further Reading section of this Pocket Guide lists some books on the history of the Navy, which provide valuable background reading. The greater your understanding of their context, the easier it is to search the records. Apart from reading the books listed below, it is also worth contacting the National Maritime Museum and the Royal Naval Museum. Both these organisations hold large collections of naval historical records including diaries, artefacts and lists.

▼ National Maritime Museum
   Maritime Information Centre
   Romney Road
   London SE10 9NF

▼ Royal Naval Museum
   HM Naval Base
   Portsmouth
   Hampshire PO1 3NH

Public Record Office (PRO)

The Public Record Office at Kew is the national repository (storehouse) for government records in the UK. It holds the records of the government departments that administered the Navy from its beginnings until the point at which the confidentiality rule applies (75 years for records containing personal information).

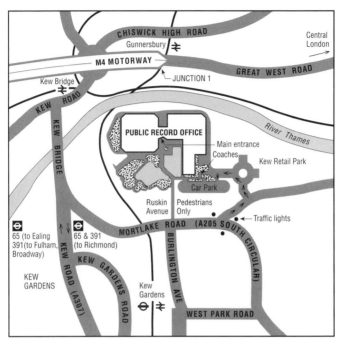

How to find the Public Record Office, Kew

What to take with you to the PRO

- £1 coin (refundable) to dump any extra baggage in a locker

- money or a credit card if you are intending to buy copies of any records

- pencil (ink and rubbers are not allowed in case they damage original records)

- paper to record what you find (notebooks are allowed, but no more than 6 loose sheets are permitted)

- a record of any research you have done so far to make sure you don't go through anything twice unnecessarily

- a laptop computer if you wish

There is also an extensive library at Kew, with a unique collection of books and periodicals on family history as well as other aspects of history.

▼ Public Record Office
Kew
Richmond
Surrey TW9 4DU
General telephone: 020 8876 3444
Telephone number for enquiries: 020 8392 5200
Telephone number for advance ordering of documents
(with exact references only): 020 8392 5260
Internet: http://www.pro.gov.uk/

Opening times (closed Sundays and Bank Holidays)

Monday	9.00 a.m. to 5 p.m.
Tuesday	10 a.m. to 7 p.m.
Wednesday	9.00 a.m. to 5 p.m.
Thursday	9.00 a.m. to 7 p.m.
Friday	9.00 a.m. to 5 p.m.
Saturday	9.30 a.m. to 5 p.m.

No appointment is needed to visit the PRO in Kew, but you will need a reader's ticket to gain access to the research areas. To obtain a ticket you need to take with you a full UK driving licence or a UK banker's card or a passport if you are a British citizen, and your passport or national identity card if you are not a British citizen. Note that the last time for ordering documents is 4 p.m. on Mondays, Wednesdays and Fridays; 4.30 p.m. on Tuesdays and Thursdays, and 2.30 p.m. on Saturdays.

Rank	Period covered	Type of record	PRO reference (where appropriate)
All ranks	Up to the 18th century	State Papers, oaths of allegiance	
Commissioned officers	From 1782	*Navy Lists*	
All officers	1756–1966*	Service records	ADM 196
All officers	1817–51	Survey returns	ADM 9, ADM 6, ADM 11
All officers	1673–1847	Succession books	ADM 6, ADM 7, ADM 11, ADM 106, ADM 76
All officers	1668–1923	Full and half pay registers	ADM 22–ADM 25, PMG 15

* Few records extend to this date. The latest date of entry in ADM 196 is 1927.

Rank	Period covered	Type of record	PRO reference (where appropriate)
All officers	1691–1902	Passing certificates	ADM 6, ADM 13, ADM 107
All officers	1759–1815	Black books	ADM 12, ADM 11
All officers	1783–1847	Leave books	ADM 6
All officers	1876–1957	Exam results	ADM 203
Officers and ratings	1854–1960s	Medal recommendations	ADM 1, ADM 116, ADM 171
Ratings	1667–1923	Ships' muster books	ADM 36–ADM 39, ADM 41, 115, 119
Ratings	1691–1856	Pay books	ADM 31–ADM 35

Rank	Period covered	Type of record	PRO reference (where appropriate)
Ratings	1853–72	Continuous Service Engagement Books	ADM 139
Ratings	1873–1923	Registers of Seamen's Services	ADM 188
Ratings and warrant officers	1802–94	Certificates of service	ADM 29, ADM 73
Ratings and warrant officers	1653–1797	Records of the Chatham Chest	ADM 82, ADM 80
Warrant officers and ratings	1694 onwards	Royal Hospital Greenwich and associated schools	ADM 73, ADM 6, RG 4, RG 8, ADM 22, 23, ADM 162–ADM 164
All officers	1809–1926	Compassionate Fund	ADM 22, ADM 23, PMG 18

Rank	Period covered	Type of record	PRO reference (where appropriate)
All officers	1836–1929	Widows' pensions	PMG 19
All officers	1830–60	Widows' claims for back pay	ADM 45
All ranks	1672–1822	Royal Bounty	ADM 16, ADM 106
Women	1917–23	Women's Royal Naval Service	ADM 318, ADM 321
All ranks	1923–39	Ministry of Defence (see p. 28)	
All ranks	1939 to present	HMS *Centurion* (see p. 28)	
All ranks	1668 onwards	Log books	ADM 53

SUMMARY OF THE RECORDS

At the Public Record Office, records are normally kept together according to the department which created them. The vast majority of records which relate to the Navy are in the Admiralty or ADM lettercode. Within the lettercode each collection, or class, of records is assigned a separate class number. Thus, most navy widows' claims for back pay are to be found in class ADM 45. It is these class numbers which are referred to throughout this Pocket Guide.

The table on p. 20–23 gives a summary of the major types of record available. For a more comprehensive list see Roger, *Naval Records for Genealogists*.

SETTING OUT

Finding the basic facts

For your search of the naval records to be successful, you need to gather as much information as possible about your ancestor. It is not generally sufficient to know only a vague date and that the Royal Navy was his profession. The surviving records about service in the Navy are fragmented and therefore difficult to search, especially those concerning service before the Continuous Service Engagement Act 1853. You need to make a careful note of what you know, to take with you. Here are a few basic questions that can help you establish a starting point:

1. **Can you find any reference to the name of a ship?**

   If you can match the name of a ship with a date when your ancestor could have been on it, you have a great starting point for your search.

2. **Was your ancestor likely to have been an officer or a rating?**

   Some of the records for officers and ratings are separate and some are combined. There are also different types of records for different types of officers so it is helpful if you know your ancestor's type of service.

3. **Was your ancestor's service likely to have been completed before 1853?**

   There were no centralised records kept for Royal Navy personnel before 1853. From 1 July 1853 details of every seaman were entered in the Continuous Service Engagement Books.

4. **What area of the country did your ancestor come from?**

   Most important ports for the Royal Navy were clustered around the eastern and southern coasts of England. These ports were where most people went to join the service, and men who lived locally to them were the most likely to have been pressed into service. Seamen would often move away to other areas of the country if they wanted to avoid the press, or sometimes would move inland.

Where to start your search

The answers to these questions should help narrow down your search into various basic categories, which are mirrored in the subject headings below. First, there are some types of record that are easier to search than others and therefore make the best starting points if they are relevant to your ancestor's period of service. These are described first.

The next brief section deals with service before 1660, for which there are very few specifically naval records. The following section describes the centralised record keeping system that was instituted when continuous service was introduced in 1853, and incidentally made tracing individuals much easier.

The next sections outline other potential lines of enquiry depending on the circumstances of the individual you are trying to trace. There are many records that are relevant only to officers or even specific types of officers. A small proportion of both officers and ratings received pensions and the pension records can reveal much detail about an individual's career and family. Women have played a small part in the history of the Royal Navy and therefore they have their own brief section.

Finally it is important not to forget that information can be gleaned from other sources within the national collection of official records. The final two sections indicate how you can find out more about the Royal Navy.

Officer's Name *Callaghan Charles*

Last Ship and Rating before Promotion, H.M.S. "Pelican" P.O. 1st Class.

500

Ship	Rank	Period of Service		Time served				REMARKS
		From	To	In Commission		In Ordinary or Reserve		
				Years at Sea Days	Days	Years at Sea Days	Days	
Boom C S No 5/83	Seaman Petty Officer		23 Dec 79	–	–	11	42	Boatswain 24 December 1879
Pelican sup S	Boatswain S	24 Dec 79	7 Feb 80					
Shannon S	"	8 Feb 80	19 June 81					
Indus 4	"	15 June 81	8 May 82					
Revenge S	"	9 May 82	8 May 83					
Indus H	"	9 May 83	3 June 85					
Leander S	"	4 June 85	4 Apl 89					
Indus S	"	5 Apl 89	31 Aug 89					
Indus H	"	1 Sept 89	3 Feb 90					
Triumph H	"	4 Feb 90	21 July 90	15	78			
Do S Manœuvre	"	22 July 90	27 Aug 90					
Do H	"	28 Aug 90	3 May 91					
Do	"	4 May 91	3 Feb 92					
Vivid (2) H	"	4 Feb 92	24 Mar 92					
Victory H	"	25 Mar 92	13 July 94					
Daphne S	"	14 July 94	15 Feb 95					
Vivid (2) H	"	16 Feb 95	7 March 95					
Pension	"	8 Mch 95	31 March 10	26 – 120				
	"	1st April 10	30 June 23					
	"	1 July 23	25 Apl 39					

Letters of Administration produced in favour
of Mrs E O'Callaghan (Administratrix) c/o Messrs.
M.L. Allen & Son (Solicitors) 1 Westbourne Place, Cobh.

Record of service for Charles Callaghan,
Petty Officer 1st Class (ADM 196/31)

SOME STRAIGHTFORWARD STARTING POINTS

For the 20th century

Records of Royal Naval personnel are kept in confidence for 75 years and can only be obtained by the next of kin. Currently the Ministry of Defence holds records of service that began after 1923. Applications for copies of the records of those whose service started between 1923 and 1939 must be made in writing giving full service details to:

▶ Ministry of Defence
  CS(R)2e
  Bourne Avenue
  Hayes
  Middlesex UB3 1RF

Next of kin only can obtain copies of records of service that began in 1939 or later by writing giving full service details to:

▶ Ministry of Defence
  PP1 A1
  HMS *Centurion*
  Grange Road
  Gosport
  Hampshire PO13 9XA

For all ranks in service in 1861

If you are sure that your ancestor was in naval service in 1861 you can look for him in the index of seamen in the 1861 census. This lists all seamen on ships both in home waters and abroad on census night. The index is available at the following address:

▼ Family Records Centre
  1 Myddelton Street
  London EC1R 1UW
  Telephone: 020 8392 5300

For commissioned officers

If your ancestor was a commissioned officer the best place to start your search for him is in the published lists available at both the PRO and many other libraries. The most important is the *Navy List*, which was started in 1782 as *Steel's Navy List*, and since 1814 has been updated quarterly as the *Navy List*. This gives officers in order of seniority with cross references to lists of officers serving on each ship. You can use it to trace the outline of an officer's career. The only gaps in the *Navy Lists* are during the First and Second World Wars, when much of the information was kept in secret. The formerly secret editions are now held at the PRO in Kew in ADM 177.

If you are lucky enough to find an ancestor who reached the highest ranks, an admiral or a captain, it is worth looking for him amongst the various available collections of biographical material including the *Dictionary of National Biography*. There is also a wealth of biographical information even about the less illustrious officers available in the specialist libraries.

Other useful published sources of information on commissioned officers include:

- Syrett and DiNardo, *The Commissioned Sea Officers of the Royal Navy, 1660–1815*

- Haultain, *The New Navy List* (containing more information than the *Navy List* for 1841–56)

- O'Byrne, *Naval Biographical Dictionary* (for all commissioned officers alive in 1846)

- *Naval Chronicle* (a newspaper for officers, which can be read at:

▶ British Library Newspaper Library
Colindale Avenue
London NW9 5HE
Telephone: 020 7412 7356

RECORDS OF NAVAL SERVICE
BEFORE 1660

The medieval navy was not a self-contained constituted body. It was largely owned by the crown and its surviving records are to be found amongst the State Papers and other governmental records. Even after the Tudors set up the Navy Board official records were not kept of individual seamen. The State Papers remain the main source of information about naval service until at least the Restoration, when in 1660 all officers and men took an oath of allegiance to Charles II. Records of those who took the oath and also of those who took a similar oath of allegiance to William III in 1696 can be searched at the PRO.

RECORDS 1853–1923

From the reorganisation of Royal Navy service in 1853 each new recruit was issued with a unique continuous service number. This applied both to new recruits to the service and to many others who transferred to the new conditions. The numbering system makes it very much easier to trace an ancestor whose service extended beyond 1853 than one whose service ended before then.

The numbering system and the types of record kept were modified several times after 1853 leaving the following different types of major records:

- **1853–72** Continuous Service Engagement Books list all recruits in numerical order of the continuous service numbers allocated. There are alphabetical name indexes to these records so it is not hard to find individual entries. The books record each seaman's date and place of birth, physical appearance and service to date.

ⓘ Remember

All continuous service numbers below 40001 are for men who enlisted before 1873.

- **1873–1923** Registers of Seamen's Services list all those already serving in 1873 and all those who enlisted in 1873 and subsequently. The men are listed in numerical order by their service numbers, but an alphabetical name index is available. Details given include dates of birth and outlines of service including the names of ships served on.

- **1894–1923** From January 1894 the continuous numbering sequence for all seamen was discontinued in favour of allocating groups of numbers to different branches of the Royal Navy. From this time you can tell which branch of the Navy your ancestor was in if you know his service number, and if you know which branch he was in but not his service number you can more easily find out what the number was. A further modification of the

Extract from the service record for rating ON121185, Richard Eaton (PRO ADM 188/157)

121185   Chatham   121185

Names in full

Richard Eaton

Date of Birth 3 June 1867.

Place of Birth Bethnal Green
                Middlesex

Date and Period of C.S. Engagement.	Ships served in. Coast Guard. Seamen Riggers.	Ships' Books. List. No.	Rating, &c.	G.C. Badges worn.	Personal Description.					Trade.	Gunnery Engagements.
					Height.	Hair.	Eyes.	Complexion.	Wounds, Scars, or Marks.		
3 June 1885 – 10 yrs.	Impregnable	15 282	3.2.6	—	4 – 10½	Brown	Blue	Fair	Anchor on left fore arm	Fis, niphilly	
28 Jany 1895 – 2o Cont. vol.				·.·	S. H.	"	"	"	"	Damenth	
	Wye	27	D.I.C.	·.·	(18)	"	"	Fresh	"		
	Ajax	15 867									
	"	10 42	Ord.								
	"	15 69	Ord.								
		TM 20.9.85									

Period of Service.		Time.		Character.	If Discharged. Whither and for what cause.	Remarks.
From	To	Years.	Days.			
85 Oct 85						H.E.
31 Oct. 85	4 July 92			·V.Y.		
5 July 92	27 July 92			V.G.S.17.01		
28 July 92						9th 5.5. Jones
3 June 85	26 Oct. 86			N.V.G.31.12.85		leave G.S. mens H.

1894–1907	Branch	1908–23
178001–240500	Seamen and communications ratings	J 1–J 110000
268001–273000	Engine room artificers	M 1–M 38000
276001–313000	Stokers	K 1–K 63500
340001–348000	Artisans and miscellaneous	M 1–M 38000
350001–352000	Sick berth staff and ship's police	M 1–M 38000
353001–366450	Officers' stewards, cooks and boy servants/stewards	L 1–L 15000
	Royal Naval Air Service (formed 1914)	Prefix F
	Short service seamen (from 1903)	Prefix SS 1
	Short service stokers (from 1903)	Prefix SS 100001

system from 1908 gave each branch of the Royal Navy its own alphabetical prefix so that you can tell from a glance at a service number which branch it belongs to. The table opposite gives the numbering sequences used.

TRACING OFFICERS

As outlined above the *Navy List* is the starting point for finding out about an officer ancestor, but this will only give you the barest outline of his career. There are also seniority lists for the highest ranks (including admirals, captains and commanders) available at the PRO and elsewhere. There are many potential sources for further information. The best are explained below. If you want to explore further you can find other lines of enquiry in Roger, *Naval Records for Genealogists*.

Officers' service registers, 1756–1966

Registers recording the naval careers of individual officers were begun in the mid-19th century. Retrospective entries were made going back to 1756, though these are not complete. The main body of the entries covers 1840–1920. Deaths are entered up until the 1950s. The information given varies from register to register but generally includes:

- names of the ships on which each officer served

- dates and places of births and deaths

- dates and places of marriages and full names of brides

There is a collection of indexes to help you find your ancestor in these registers. Do not give up too easily if you cannot find your ancestor's name in the expected index as they are of variable reliability. You may also find entries for your ancestor in more than one register because different departments of the Admiralty compiled different registers.

There are also registers of confidential performance reports by commanding officers on captains and flag officers hoping to be promoted to the rank of admiral. These give real insight into the individual men.

Survey returns, 1817–51

The Admiralty conducted a series of surveys of officers, starting in 1817. The purpose of the surveys was to improve record keeping in order to gain a clearer picture of the state of the Navy after the conclusion of the Napoleonic wars in 1815. A range of surveys was conducted covering both commissioned officers and warrant officers. The collection of returns is far from complete because of the numbers of officers who never received their survey

284. 331. 443. 4/36. 381. 7/12. 46 314. 331. —7/144.

K2 528

27

Ships	Entry	Quality	Discharge	Time			
				Y.	M.	W.	D.
Culloden	20 Apl 1805	Midshipmn Lieut	23 July 06	1	3	1	4
Rattlesnake	25 July 06	Actg Com	19 Sept 06	—	2	0	1
Perseverance	20 Sept 06	Actg Capt	1 June 07	—	9	0	3
Psyche	2 June 07	..	11 Oct 07	—	4	2	6
Powerful	12 Oct 07	..	18 Feb 08	—	4	2	4
Cornwallis	19 Feb 08	..	5 July 08	—	4	3	5
Phaeton	6 July 08	Vict	15 Aug 12	4	1	1	6
Iphigenia	11 Novt 12	Capt	31 Jan 13	—	2	3	5
Resistance	1 Feb 13	..	7 Feb 14	1	0	1	0
Revolutionaire	25 Augt 18	..	5 July 22	3 11	1	0

Indefatigable	18 Feby 96	Vol	20 Feby 99				
Impetueux	18 Nov 99	Vol Jan	14 Oct 1800				
Do	1 May 01	as	15 Apl 02				
Tonnant	17 Mch 03	Mid	8 May 04				
Culloden	9 May 04	—	19 Apl 05				

ADMIRALTY,   18 Sept   18 43

These are to Certify, That Capt the Honble Sir F.B.R. Pellew M. &c. K.C.M.

is borne on the Books of Her Majesty's Ships above-mentioned the Time and in the Qualities

there expressed, being

For
Lieut. 8 Sept 1805.
Comt. 12 Oct 07.
Capt. 14 Oct 08.

Commissioned officer's service record for Fleetwood
Broughton Reynolds Pellew (PRO ADM 196/5)

letters and the numbers who never replied. Indexes are available to parts of the survey collection.

Succession books, 1673–1847

Each ship kept a succession book to record the names in succession of those who held each officer position. These books are useful in providing a means to trace an officer from one ship to another. It can be done simply because there are name indexes. The series of succession books are as follows:

- commissioned and warrant officers, 1673–88

- admirals, captains and commanders, 1688–1725

- masters, surgeons, surgeons' mates, sailmakers and others, 1733–55 and 1770–1807

- pursers, gunners, boatswains, carpenters and some dockyard officers, 1764–1831 and 1800–39

- junior officers appointed by the Admiralty, 1699–1824

Officers' full and half pay registers, 1668–1924

These are the records of salary payments made to officers. The full pay registers are not very informative, giving only the name of each officer and the sum paid, but they are useful as a means of confirming periods of active service. There is a separate register for each commissioned rank between 1795 and 1830. After 1830 all ranks were registered together.

Officers were put on half pay as a retainer between engagements on ship and half pay also came to act rather like a pension, with some officers who were no longer fit for service being retained on half pay for years. The half pay registers are often useful in providing addresses to which the pay was sent. Early half pay records (1668–89) were made in Bill Books and are difficult to search because they were not compiled in any particular order. After 1836 the registers are easier to follow because they were either compiled in alphabetical order or have indexes.

The full and half pay registers were used to compile certificates of service for warrant officers who applied for naval pensions. Certificates of service are described below because they were mostly issued to ratings rather than officers.

Passing certificates, 1691–1902

These records consist of three series of certificates issued
to prove the qualifications of officers including:

- lieutenants
- warrant officers
- engineers

The certificates gave a summary of each officer's service
and training and some have records of baptism or birth
certificates attached to prove the officer's age. There are
also examination registers for those hoping to become lieutenants, 1795–1832, which give the candidates' names,
ages and a record of qualifying service. There is a partial
index for the certificates and others are arranged alphabetically by year, making searching relatively easy if you
have an approximate year.

Warrant officers

The status of warrant officers has evolved greatly during
the history of the Royal Navy, with some types of warrant
officers achieving commissioned status as follows:

- masters in 1808
- pursers and surgeons in 1843
- engineers in 1847

The ranks of junior warrant officers continually expanded until there were twenty-four different branches in 1945. If you are looking for an ancestor who was a warrant officer it is worth finding out the exact type if you can, as this will help you find your way through the fragmented records. A full discussion of this issue can be found in Rodger, *Naval Records for Genealogists*.

There are some records which are relevant only to specialist types of warrant officer. These are listed in the table on p. 42–3.

Finding further details

Once you have traced an outline of your ancestor's career as a naval officer, there are numerous potential sources to search for more information. The means of promotion in the Navy was so involved that it required a great deal of paperwork, with recommendations travelling around the world in the hope of securing a position for a protégé. To find these it is worth searching through private papers and the notebooks of the First Lords and First Naval Lords of the Admiralty. Here you will find personal comment that is mostly absent from the official record. It might also be worth looking among the confidential assessments made annually from the mid-19th century by commanding officers on all officers under their command, though unfortunately few of these survive.

Type of warrant officer	Type of record	PRO reference (where appropriate)
All warrant officers	Black books recording misconduct, 1741–1814	ADM 11
Boatswains, gunners and carpenters	Service registers, 1848–90	ADM 196
Boatswains	Passing certificates, 1810–13, 1851–5, 1856–9, 1860–87	ADM 6, ADM 13
Chaplains	Published book: *Sea Chaplains*	
Chaplains	Full records kept by the Chaplain of the Fleet	
Engineers	Service registers, 1837–86	ADM 196, ADM 29
Gunners	Passing certificates, 1731–48, 1760–97, 1803–12	ADM 6

Type of warrant officer	Type of record	PRO reference (where appropriate)
Masters	Passing certificates, 1660–1830	ADM 106
Masters	Service records, 1800–50 1848–82	ADM 6, ADM 196
Pursers (later known as paymasters)	Candidates for promotion, 1803–4, 1847–54	ADM 6, ADM 11
Pursers (later known as paymasters)	Passing certificates, 1813–20, 1851–67, 1868–89	ADM 6, ADM 13
Pursers (later known as paymasters)	Service registers, 1843–1922	ADM 196, ADM 6
Surgeons	Passing certificates, 1700–1800	ADM 106
Surgeons	Service registers, 1774–86	ADM 104
Surgeons	Reports on pay and promotion, 1817–32	ADM 105

Other sources of details include:

- black books, 1759–1815, recording misconduct and dismissal from the service

- leave books, 1783–1847, recording leave granted to officers

- examination results from the Royal Naval College, Greenwich, 1876–1957

- recommendations for gallantry medals first awarded during the Crimean War

- wills submitted by officers' widows in claims for repayment of back pay, 1830–60

- registers of those officers who were unfit for service

TRACING RATINGS

Ships' musters and pay books, 1667–1878

A muster is a list of everyone in the crew aboard ship – the ship's company. Musters were compiled for each ship in the service of the crown from medieval times, though unfortunately most musters compiled before 1685 were burnt in a fire in that year on board the *Eagle*, the hulk on which they were stored. Before the Continuous Service Engagement Books were begun in 1853, ships' musters and pay books are the chief source for tracing the career of a seaman below the rank of officer.

Musters named all the crew and from 1764 gave the ages of seamen on boarding the ship and places of birth of most. They recorded the service of each seaman accurately for the purpose of paying him and also kept a check of the amounts to be deducted from his pay for food and services on board. They were a complex and detailed type of record. They did not usually form a continuous record for a voyage, since if payment was made to the crew part way through a long voyage, they were 'split', with a new record beginning a new payment period. For this reason musters typically cover a period of six months or a year.

ⓘ Remember
Men came and went from ships during voyages for many reasons including being lent to other ships and being left behind if they fell sick. It is worth searching all the lists on each muster that might include your ancestor.

In order to search these musters effectively you need to have a ship's name and a date, otherwise there are just too many to trawl through. If you find your ancestor in one muster book, it may not make it easier to trace him to another because until 1853 he was likely to be discharged from the ship he was on at the end of its commission into the community. On the other hand he will be easier to trace if he:

- returned to the same ship

- served on another ship at the same port

- served with the same captain on another ship

- was part of a crew turned over directly to another Royal Navy ship (as was usually the case in wartime)

Tips for finding the name of the ship your ancestor was on:

- If you know where your ancestor was on a specific date, check in the Naval List Books (from 1673) to find which ships were at the nearest port on that date and search the musters for those ships.

- Check the certificates of service issued by the Navy Pay Office, 1790–1865, to those wishing to apply for assistance. These list ships served on (see pp. 47–9).

From about 1800 some musters included description books for the men. These recorded a careful description of the appearance of each individual for identification purposes in case of death or desertion.

Pay books (1691–1856) were kept separately from the musters as records of payments made. They contain much of the same information as the musters with some further details and frequent later additions as further payments were made. Another addition from 1765, which makes them a very useful source to search, was the 'alphabets' or list of names in alphabetical order.

Certificates of service, 1802–94

A certificate of service was an outline of an individual seaman's career that named all the ships he served on with dates and gave a total of paid service. The certificates were compiled by the Navy Pay Office from ships' pay books. They were used to support applications for:

- pensions
- gratuities and medals
- admission to the Greenwich Hospital
- admission of seamen's children into the Greenwich Hospital School

---

ⓘ Remember
You can use the ships' pay books to compile your own record for your ancestor similar to a certificate of service.

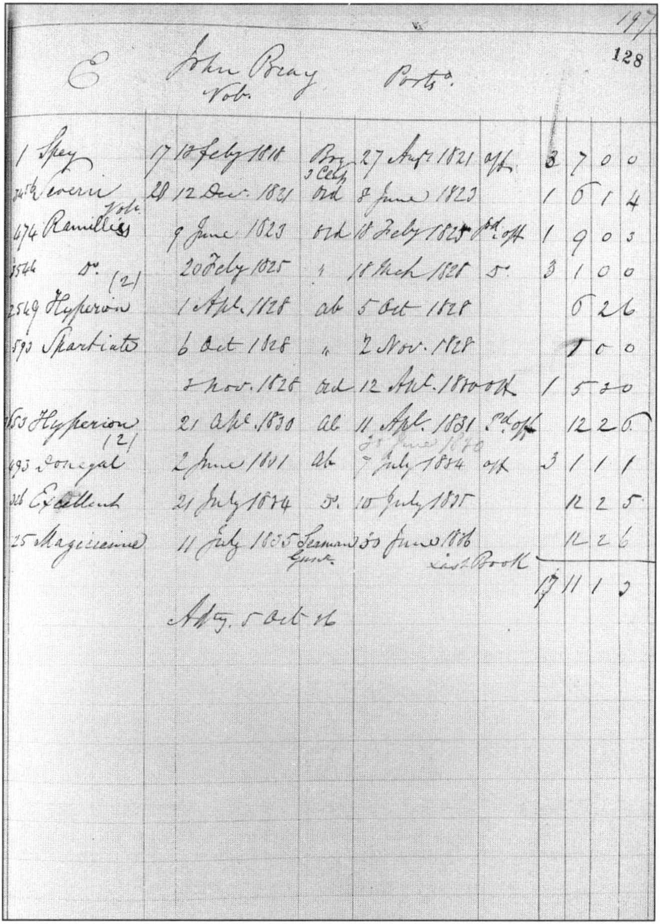

E John Bray Vob. Ports.

197 128

1 Spey	17	10 Feby 1818	Boy 3 Class	27 Augt 1821	off	3	7	0	0
745 Leveret	28	12 Decr 1821	Ord	8 June 1823		1	6	1	4
474 Ramillies Vob.		9 June 1823	Ord	18 Feby 1825	Pd off	1	9	0	3
1546 Do. (2)		20 Feby 1825	"	18 Mch 1828	Do.	3	1	0	0
2549 Hyperion		1 Apl 1828	Ab	5 Oct 1828			6	2	6
593 Spartiate		6 Oct 1828	"	2 Nov. 1828			1	0	0
		3 Nov. 1828	Ord	12 Apl. 1830	off	1	5	3	0
1153 Hyperion (2)		21 Apl 1830	Ab	11 Apl. 1831	Pd off		12	2	0
493 Donegal		2 June 1831	Ab	7 July 1834	off	3	1	1	1
326 Excellent		21 July 1834	Do.	10 July 1835			12	2	5
25 Magicienne		11 July 1835	Seaman Gunr	30 June 1836	List Book		12	2	6
						17	11	1	3

Adty. 5 Oct 36

Pre-1853 rating's service record, for John Bray, showing a pension granted to him by the Admiralty, 5 October 1836 (PRO ADM 29/13)

See also p. 31–5 for seamen's records.

The dates when the certificates were issued are given in the certificates of service books rather than the date when service ended. Many of these certificates were issued after the death of a seaman or even while a seaman was still in service in order to secure the care of his children.

Until 1834 pensions were rarely given to ranks below warrant officer so that for ordinary seamen you are more likely to find a certificate after 1834 than before.

PENSION RECORDS

The Royal Navy was slow to introduce pension entitlements to the men in its service. Automatic pensions for ratings were not introduced until 1853, when they became entitled to a pension after twenty years' service. Unfortunately few records of these pensions survive. Before 1853 there was a range of pensions and other forms of relief available both to the seamen themselves and to their families, but only a few of the most needy received them. Some pensions were specifically for those who were wounded or achieved honour in battle, or medals. The records of these pensions are as numerous and varied as the pensions were themselves, but they remain the best source available for tracing the families of men in the Royal Navy. If you do find your ancestors you should gain some solid information about them since proof of births, marriages and deaths in the form of certificates was generally required as part of an application for assistance. You will also find out a great deal about the precarious existence of a naval family.

Pension provision for officers was sometimes separate and sometimes in common with provision for ordinary seamen, depending on the level of need. Pensions were available for fixed numbers of the most senior officers – from 1672 for warrant officers, 1737 for lieutenants, and 1747 for admirals. Half pay was also used as a pension provision (see p. 39). More universal pensions for officers were introduced from the mid-1830s. From 1862 those officers who wished their wives to be eligible for widows' pensions were required to place copies of their marriage certificates on file. Details from the certificates were entered in service registers and a small collection of the actual certificates together with a name index is held at the PRO.

The sections below describe a selection of the most accessible pension records available. For a full list see Rodger, *Naval Records for Genealogists*.

The Chatham Chest

The first provision of aid for dependants of men who had served in the Royal Navy was set up around 1590, and known as the Chatham Chest. This was a charitable institution funded by sixpence deducted from the pay of seamen serving in the Navy. There was no automatic entitlement to aid from the Chatham Chest, and only the most deserving cases benefited.

The chief beneficiaries from the Chatham Chest were the families of warrant officers until 1834, when more money was made available to the families of ratings. In order to receive help it was necessary to gather a range of documents to prove the worthiness of the cause. The most important of these documents was the certificate of service (see p. 47–9), which was a record of service rendered.

ⓘ Remember
It was only the lucky few who gained assistance from the charitable provisions of the 17th and 18th centuries.

The records of the Chatham Chest include:

- account books, 1653–7

- registers of payments to pensioners, 1675–1799 (including annual alphabetical lists)

- pension indexes, 1744–97, linking names of seamen to the ships on which they served

The Royal Greenwich Hospital, 1694–1869

The Royal Greenwich Hospital was set up in the late 17th century and funded throughout most of the period until 1869 by sixpence deducted from every seaman's wage, including merchant seamen, though they were seldom beneficiaries. It provided accommodation for the most deserving of the wounded and infirm and employment for seamen's widows as nurses. In order to be admitted seamen had to present their case and the papers relating to applications made between 1737 and 1859 survive. Other important surviving records include:

- entry books, 1704–1869

- admission papers, 1790–1865

- church registers from the hospital, 1705–1864 (giving details mainly of deaths)

The hospital also made payments to registered out-patients living throughout the British Isles and abroad. Most of these out-patients had formerly been in the lower ranks of the Navy. There were a thousand pensioners by 1738 and 2,350 by 1782. During the 19th century more and more officers became recipients. Out-patient records include:

- registers of applicants, 1789–1859

- pay books, 1781–1809, and arranged alphabetically, 1814–46

- registers of officers receiving payments, 1814, 1815–42, 1846–1921

The Royal Hospital School, Greenwich, was set up shortly after the hospital itself, for the education of sons of seamen. Priority was given to the children of men who had been killed or wounded in Royal Navy service, though the admittance of the children of commissioned officers became rare. This school admitted boys at 13 years old, but in 1805 the Royal Naval Asylum was set up for younger orphans and boys from this school frequently progressed to the main school. The two schools were amalgamated in 1821 and a separate school was established for the sons of commissioned officers.

The records of the various schools include:

- admission papers, 1728–1870 (certificates proving birth, the parents' marriage and the father's naval service)

- registers of applications, 1728 onwards

- church registers (mainly of deaths)

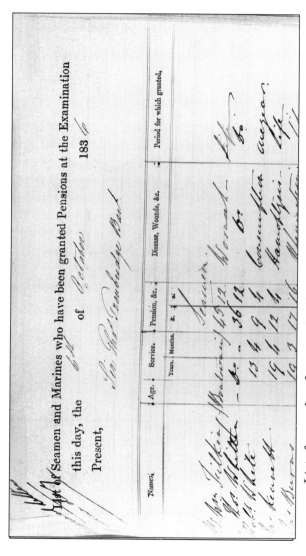

List of men who after examination were granted a pension or gratuity by Royal Greenwich Hospital, 6 October 1836 (PRO ADM 6/297)

Charity for the Payment of Pensions to Officers' Widows

This was a fund established in 1732 from a combination of parliamentary grants and deductions from officers' pay. It paid pensions to widows of commissioned and warrant officers on the basis of need, although the terms of payments varied from time to time. The surviving records of this fund include:

- pay books, 1734–1835, 1836–1929

- application papers, 1797–1829 (including many marriage and death certificates)

- applications requiring further investigation, 1808–30

There is a partial index to the application papers.

Pensions administered by the Admiralty

The Admiralty was responsible for a range of pensions paid to officers and their families. The first were paid from 1673 to the widows of officers who died in action. In 1809 a Compassionate Fund was set up for orphans and dependants of officers and from 1830 Admiralty pensions were paid to the officers' widows. The Admiralty also administered the Royal Bounty, which was a lump sum equivalent to an officer's annual salary paid to his widow.

The records of these various pensions and others include pay books and registers of applications, which give brief details of the officers' careers and include marriage, birth and death certificates.

Pensions for the disabled

Many of the pensions described above were available to the wounded but a separate collection is held at the PRO of a sample of 5000 disabled seamen and soldiers in receipt of disablement pensions before 1914. The sample includes their personal files, which contain details of injuries suffered, medical records and their own accounts of what happened. The records in this sample are arranged alphabetically by name.

WOMEN AND THE ROYAL NAVY

The role of women in the Royal Navy has been slight until very recently. Widows of seamen were employed for a while at the Royal Greenwich Hospital, as mentioned on p. 52, but no women were ever employed on ship. Women were employed by the Royal Navy as nurses but this practice ceased for much of the 19th century. It restarted in 1883 with the establishment of the professional Naval Nursing Sisters, who became known as Queen Alexandra's Royal Naval Nursing Service in 1902. Head nursing sisters, as the highest rank of women, were included in the *Navy Lists* from 1884 and other nurses of officer rank were included from 1890. Service records for nurses, 1884–1918, and succession books, 1921–39, are held by the PRO under class reference ADM 104.

There was no Women's Royal Naval Service until 1917, and because of the 75 year rule of confidentiality few records of this service are available. There are some personal records available for women serving between 1917 and 1918 and registers of appointments, promotions and resignations.

OTHER RELEVANT
OFFICIAL RECORDS

There are various types of official record unconnected with the Royal Navy that can yield information about a seaman's life. These are explained below.

Records of births, marriages and deaths

Civil registration of births, marriages and deaths at sea was introduced in 1851, though some registers pre-date this. The Office of National Statistics holds those registers of births, marriages and deaths that came into the possession of the Registrar General through the civil registration system. Indexes to these registers can be searched at the Family Records Centre at the address on p. 29. The relevant indexes to records held here include:

- Births and deaths at sea registered from July 1837 to 1965

- Royal Naval returns of births, marriages and deaths from 1959

- First World War naval deaths, 1914–21

- Second World War naval deaths, 3 September 1939 to 30 June 1948

Censuses

The census was a survey of the entire population of the British Isles taken every ten years from 1801. Until 1841 the census was just a headcount and yielded little of interest to family historians. For the 1841 census and thereafter captains had a duty to complete a census return giving standard information for everyone on board their ship on census night. The heads of large institutions, such as the Royal Greenwich Hospital, had the same obligation.

The easiest census to search is that of 1861, as explained on p. 29, but it might also be worth checking the 1881 census because it has an alphabetical name index. The original census returns are closed to the general public for a hundred years so the latest available census for searching will be that of 1891 until the year 2002.

Wills

The Admiralty collected a large number of copies of seamen's wills during the course of administering pensions, grants and applications by their dependants for the back pay of men killed in service. The majority of Admiralty records relevant to wills can be found in the PRO under the class references ADM 142, ADM 48, ADM 44 and ADM 45.

The proving of most seamen's wills was done until 1815 by the Prerogative Court of the Archbishop of Canterbury. Officially this court was responsible for all wills of seamen who died with at least £20 owing in back pay. Its records are also held at the PRO in Kew. After 1858 a central probate court was instituted for the proving of all wills, including those of men serving in the Royal Navy. See the Pocket Guide *Using Wills* to find out how to search wills records.

LIFE AT SEA

Once you have traced an outline of your ancestor's career there are many further interesting records to research that do not often mention individuals but do vividly evoke their lives. The chief of these is the ships' logs, which survive from around 1688. If you can find the ship's log of the ship on which your ancestor served, it will give you an account of where the ship sailed and what day-to-day life on board was like. Ships' logs were kept by captains, masters and lieutenants.

Another interesting source is the surgeons' records. These recount the constant battle with sickness that was waged on board ship. The cramped conditions and poor diet caused a range of diseases from scurvy to tuberculosis. It was also common for men to pick up more exotic diseases ashore, especially venereal disease. The gruelling work of manning the ship caused a range of injuries, for which, often, little could be done.

Lastly there are huge collections of private and official papers to discover. There are diaries kept by captains and admirals and accounts of battles and voyages. There are assessments of men and strategic plans. There are maps of the high seas and lists of medals. There is enough scope for a lifetime of study!

Name	Rank or Rating	No.	Medals, &c., earned			How Issued or disposed of	Remarks
1	2	3	4			5	6
CORNWELL, Fredk.G.	J.R.A.	M.32786			B.	S.	
" Fredk.J.	Sto.2.	K.50040		V	B.	S.	
" Fredk.W.	L.M.	F.23819		V	B.	By A.M.	
" Harvey A.	Ord.	J.56797			B.	F.	R.
" Henry A.	Ord.	J.50226		V	B.	S.	
" Herbert	A.B.	S.S.3551	St	V	B.	MR.	I.C. 2000/1920.
" Herbert=Fld.	Sto.2.	K.53698			B.	S.	
" Jas.L.	2 S.B.S.	M.8361	St	V	B.	S.	Def. 9157 30/9/41.
" Job	A.B.	161530	St	V	B.	S.	
" John E.	Act. S.P.O.	365797	St	V	B.	S.	
" John J.	L.M.	F.13058			B.	S.	
" John T. V.C.	Boy 1.	J.42563		V	B.	BR.	I.C. 692/1916.
" John W.	C.P.O.	187472	St	V	B.	S.	
" John W.	Ord.	J.87790		Y	B.	"Wallflower."	
" Sidney J.M.	B.Art.	M.22628			B.	"Conquest."	
" Walter	S.B.A.	M.16786			B.	S.	
" Wm.E.	O.Tel.	J.55420		V	B.	"Vernon."	
" Wm.F.	Ord.	J.63548		V	B.	S.	
" Wm.G.	A.B.	J.70351		V	B.	S.	
CORONEL, Samuel H.	A.C.1.	F.27126			B.		
CORONEO, Demetrius	A.C.1.	F.20135			B.		
CORP, Geo.W.	Sto.1.	K.18718	St	V	B.	"Espiegle."	
" Oliver	Sto.1.	K.4561	St	V	B.	"Impregnable."	
" Richmond	Ch.Sto.	280271	St	V	B.	S.	
" Wm.J.	Act. A.M.1.	F.34401			B.	S.	

First World War naval medal roll (ADM 171/99)

FURTHER READING

J. Campbell and W. Stevenson, *Lives of the British Admirals* (London, 1917)

K. Douglas-Morris, *The Naval General Service Medal, 1793–1840* (Margate, 1982)

K. Douglas-Morris, *Naval Long Service Medals* (Bourne Press, 1991)

J.R. Hill, ed. *The Oxford Illustrated History of the Royal Navy* (Oxford University Press, 1995)

G. Taylor, *Sea Chaplains* (Oxford Illustrated Press, 1978)

London Gazette, available at the PRO and other libraries

W.R. O'Byrne, *Naval Biographical Dictionary* (London, 1849)

N.A.M. Rodger, *The Admiralty* (Lavenham, 1979)

N.A.M. Rodger, *Naval Records for Genealogists* (PRO, 1998)

D. Syrett and R.L. DiNardo, *The Commissioned Sea Officers of the Royal Navy, 1660–1815* (Navy Records Society, 1994)

A. Trotman, 'The Royal Naval Museum, Portsmouth: Genealogy at the King Alfred Library and Reading Room', *Genealogists Magazine*, vol. XXIV, pp 197–9